Fresh Focus Embracing Your New Normal
Breaking Down The Steps To True Transformation
ISBN 978-0-9960498-8-7
Copyright © 2020 by Marguerite Wormley

Printed in the United States of America
All rights reserved.
This book or any portion thereof may not be reproduced or used in any manner whatsoever without the express written permission of the publisher except for the use of brief quotations in a book review.

Preface

Everyone sometime in their lifespan will experience a new normal. Whether it's a loss of a loved one, loss of a job, health challenge or divorce to name a few, these circumstances will cause an unexpected change in an individual's life. Some people have many challenges adapting to what is now called their new normal due to circumstances that may not be their fault at all. This causes people to stay in the victim mindset and can make it difficult to move on.

This devotional book candidly discusses the process and what it involves to embrace your new normal. Over the years I had the pleasure to listen to people in particularly women who shared their losses, heartaches or experience with chronic illness. Most of their responses were not from a place of victory or acceptance but from defeat, depression, anger and bitterness.

I was inspired to write this book from listening, counseling and praying helping those to deal with the distress seasons in their life and how to move forward. These people were Sister(s) in Christ, stay at home mother's, co-workers, Pastor wife's, entrepreneurs, cashiers at retail stores and restaurants, and also close friends and family. I've learned there is nothing new under the sun, (Ecclesiastes 1:9), it's just our response to it.

Your 31 Day Walk

Day 1. Reaching Beyond the Break
Day 2. The Affliction
Day 3. The Panic Button
Day 4. Assessing the Damage
Day 5. Handling its Reality
Day 6. His Strength and His Power
Day 7. All My Worship
Day 8. Cut Above the Rest
Day 9. The Turning Point
Day 10. Hiding in Plain Sight
Day 11. It's a Pre-Mature Set-up
Day 12. The Vantage Point
Day 13. Swallow the Pill and Keep it Moving
Day 14. It Only Takes One Bite
Day 15. Not Bitter - Just Better
Day 16. The Monkey Bar Syndrome
Day 17. The Pause Button
Day 18. It's Not Easy Being You
Day 19. Know Your Worth
Day 20. Vessel of Honor
Day 21. R.E.S.P.E.C.T. Yourself
Day 22. Inner Healing Brings a Fresh Focus
Day 23. The Beauty of Waiting
Day 24. Waiting to be Blessed
Day 25. Hurry Up and Wait
Day 26. The Power of Obedience While Waiting
Day 27. Pending Status
Day 28. Grow Where God Plants You
Day 29. Fresh Focus
Day 30. Be Still
Day 31. Living My Best Life

Reaching Beyond the Break

Some adversity can appear without warning. Our lives can be at peace one moment and then a raging sea the very next moment. When life brings an unexpected change, it can drain you of all your spiritual, physical and mental energy. There's no time to ponder, think or feel things out rationally, because the hit or change can be so devastating, it will take your breath away. When you can see adversity coming you can prepare for it, in some ways, and yet it can still be a difficult process, but at least you can see it coming. To expect adversity is one thing, but not to see it coming takes things to another level.

Without any warning so much pain, shock, denial and lots of emotions are involved that could either build or destroy a person's character. In life we learn that adversity appears in several forms. It could appear in the sudden loss of a job –with gainful employment, mind you. One day you report to work and prepare to handle whatever that day brings, then immediately, you are called into the office and told you are laid off or fired. It can appear through the sudden death of a loved one --either violently or by an illness. Every day you see them, and you speak with them and then, one day they are no longer with you. Adversity can appear in an unexpected health crisis. You feel stronger and healthier than ever; you make an appointment for a routine visit and the doctor recommends that you take a specific test or tests. The test results return showing something positive with a diagnosis of some sort of life or death terminal illness that gives you little or no hope for survival. Adversity can also appear through a divorce. After spending years with a person, one of the spouses decide they no longer want to be married. This can cause the other spouse to feel vulnerable, rejected, isolated and alone because life, as they once knew, no longer exists.

Adversity comes in so many ways; these are just some of the most common scenarios people face. But, one thing they all have in common is that in midst of difficulty, they have no other choice other than to rebuild their lives and start anew.

~True Story~

My personal experience with adversity has been with the diagnosis of breast cancer, then, two years later having to except and face my failed marriage of 22 years. Having to grasp my new reality of life was extremely difficult. I didn't know how to reach beyond the shock, the pain, the disappointment, the rejection, and the embarrassment. Many people have suggested that I move on but how; how do you move on? How do you reach beyond what is no longer available? I felt so alone, along with so many identifiable emotions, as well as feeling as if I was the only one going through these adverse situations. This continued for a while, and then, many other women came across my path who had gone through similar situations and they also experienced the humiliation, the pain and devastating lost. This is when I received comfort in knowing that my God is able, and He had this…

~Here's the Thing…~

Everyone responds differently to bad news. Some may cry, some may be angry or even feel numb once the bad news has been released. You can have people around you who may be familiar with both you and the circumstance, but they just don't know what to say. Try to remember that you are not alone, and you are not the only one battling or suffering from that unfortunate circumstance. One thing about reaching out is that eventually the goal of what someone is reaching for will be accomplished. To reach out is an ongoing process that may involve some stretching that's uncomfortable. If you are reaching out for healing, peace, joy, love etc., keep reaching out and endure the stretch. You will eventually grab all that God has planned for you.

In a Place Called There…

The Affliction

Experiencing pain and suffering would allow an individual to do an evaluation of themselves. There are times when God will allow bad things to happen to get our attention, causing us to stop, look and listen. Pain and suffering can cause us to become vulnerable and they can give the enemy an open door, opportunity to our souls to bring illusions, making things seem worse than a normal process or impossibility. No one enjoys feeling vulnerable, susceptible to weakness and not having answers or knowing what to do or say. Having to face hurtful situations can cause what lies dormant within us to be revealed.

~True Story~

With my circumstance the divorce was not the painful part. It was the series of events leading up to the divorce. My marriage was not by any means perfect and we had our share of problems, which were pretty much normal, for the most part. However, the pain began subtly, when I was first made aware that our marriage was over.

After battling breast cancer, I was informed by my ex-spouse that he no longer wanted to be married. Once receiving the news, I was in total denial and I believed this was just a phase and that things would shortly get back on track after we did whatever we needed to do to save our marriage. As time went by and no favorable or positive changes were taking place or improvements, the pain became more unbearable. I cried day and night, getting no rest, having no appetite to eat and all the while, trying to function as normal as possible. This went on for about three years. This process was far more difficult than facing breast cancer. The pain I experienced and the circumstances that was unfolding before my eyes became unbearable.

~Here's the Thing...~

When it comes to pain, whether it's physical or emotional, people like your loved ones and friends, have a tendency to put a timeframe on your progress. Everyone handles pain differently. The important thing to remember is how to respond to it all. When dealing with pain, as with any other injury, there should be evidence of some healing over a process of time. Some injuries may heal slower than others but at least there is a healing taking place of some kind, and hopefully we get to see even the smallest of improvements. However, in order to get through the healing process, some pain is involved. You must confront and deal with the discomfort. If the injury is not healing properly that's when a specialist will get involve, with an effort to try and resolve our issues and concerns.

Learn to respect the pain you are experiencing. If it hurt, it hurts. Don't try to portray being stronger than you really are for people who are consistently around you to feel better about your pain –the pain you are experiencing.

Remember this:
Psalm 56:8 (NLT) "You keep track of all my sorrows. You have collected all my tears in your bottle. You have recorded each one in your book."

In a Place Called There…

The Panic Button

A panic button (a security device), is used for the purpose of alarming someone when there is an emergency. It's a call for immediate help. The device is generally connected to an alarm security system to the police or some sort of emergency personnel. When the panic button has been activated the next set of instructions will be to observe your surroundings, get to a safe place and wait for help.

As we go through life and we see and witness others misfortunes or their unfortunate experience, we silently feel bad for them, but we often wonder, in the back of our minds, what would we do if that particular situation happened to us. Normally something traumatic occurs unexpected. If trauma was to come to us, announced in advance, there would never be a need for a panic button to be created. When something approaches unexpectedly, after being shaken and stunned, now here comes the panic. The panic is there because this is not a drill where you are witnessing someone else's traumatic event --this is your own.

Once you push the panic button you are desperate to grab onto whatever you can to keep from being destroyed. The only problem is that you must be careful, and you must be strategic. The very thing you grab and hold onto may not be strong enough or it can stabilize you and end up causing destruction anyway. It's vital that after you push the panic button to be calm, observe your surroundings, get into a safe place and wait for help. It's a tough place being in a position of not knowing who or what to trust. However, the right help will be sent from God and He will make sure the help is from Him and not a setup from the enemy.

~Here's the Thing...~

When there is turmoil, gossip, accusations and confusion involved you don't know who you can trust. People, the very ones you thought could be trusted, turn on you, while others who have a neutral opinion have been influenced by what they heard or saw. I found in my experience that God will protect His own if you obey and follow His voice. Everyone who was around me was not in my favor. My family lived many miles away, so they were not around me during this time. In fact, the area where I lived while this trial was brewing was not to my advantage. During this time God surrounded me with someone who I could be transparent with; their responsibility to me was to give me the truth of God's Word and the directions from the Lord that I couldn't hear, or I wouldn't receive for myself, in that season. If you are a believer and the odds are against you unfairly, I tell you, God will come and provide the help you need.

Remember this:

2 Thessalonians 3:3 (NKJV) "But the Lord is faithful, and He will strengthen you and protect you from the evil one."

In a Place Called There…

Assessing the Damage

Anything of value that has experienced some type of damage must be assessed. Dependent upon the extent of the damage caused, it could either be repaired or, declared a total loss. Let's consider valued items; they usually have insurance placed on them. Once an inquiry for a claim has been submitted by the insured and the adjuster is scheduled to come and assess what was damaged, i.e., the cost to repair the damage and the time frame needed to complete the repair, etc., also, there is what is called a medical injury; the physician assesses the damage and then the physician decides on the necessary treatment.

One of the most difficult things to repair is a broken heart. Many things are produced from our hearts. Things like love, issues of life, trust, passion and compassion, sympathy or empathy, consideration, and so on. Well, when the heart is broken these things cannot effectively flow within your heart. In order to know how much repair, the heart needs from the hurt experienced, the first thing needed is to understand the damage. Some hurts can cost us our dignity and pride, while other hurts can cost us our self-esteem, self-worth and our morals.

When the damage has been fully assessed, then now it's time to put a treatment plan together on how to clean up or replace things as much as possible, so that the healing can begin.

Cleaning up can be a process. Everyone has their own way of cleaning and their favorite cleaning products to use because that is what has been proven to work effectively for them. The process route to receive healing from hurts and a broken heart, the following are ways or means I have found very effective, which contributed to my healing. They are:

- *Get in the Word of God*; study God's Word –don't just read it but confess His Word and mediate–breathe upon His Word, continually.

- *Surround yourself with encouraging people* with encouraging words and read encouraging and uplifting books. In fact, why not get a new circle of friends. It's very refreshing to surround yourself with people who know nothing about you or your past.

- *Change your location*, i.e., physically relocate from your old area which is a reminder of the sadness and the hurt. If the hurt is so intense that wherever you go reminds you of the past in a surrounding vicinity or locality, then it may be difficult to move on, so you may have to leave the area all together.

- *Psychologically* relocate, which is to change your thinking which will give you a new perception of things.

- *Spiritually relocate*. This does not mean to necessarily relocate to another place of worship, but to truly, deeply seek the Lord with your whole heart. Sometimes we must find God in a place called there. "Drink from the brook and eat what the ravens bring you, for I have commanded them to bring you food." 1 Kings 17:4 (NLT)

Remember this:

Isaiah 43:19 (ESV) "Behold, I am doing a new thing; now it springs forth, do you not perceive it? I will make a way in the wilderness and rivers in the desert."

In a Place Called There…

Handling its Reality

At some point in our lives all of us will face some sort of adversity. The question is how will we handle its reality? There are two ways adversity can affect a person. It can affect us in both a positive way and in a negative way.

When adversity is processed in a positive way it will guide an individual into spiritual and emotional growth. This produces maturity. However, when adversity is processed in a negative way this causes an individual to become bitter; succumbing to defeat, and most often than not, it can and will, destroy the individual.

When adversity strikes, usually it's only for a season. When you are experiencing extreme pain, it can seem like its forever and you will never stop hurting. When the season of adversity presents itself, there is no other choice but to just go through the process. You can't sing the season away, you can't pray it away, you can't praise it away, you can't manipulate it away, or give it a dollar amount; adversity must complete its cycle.

~True Story~

After receiving the news that my marriage was over, I remember thinking that I hadn't realized that things were as bad as they were. Initially, our family had entered a season of prosperity and success. I thought everything was going well. The kids were growing up and off to college; we were able to build our first home from the ground up and we even pastored a church; and we had other business endeavors on the horizon. These wonderful things were going well for us, all at the same time and it appeared that we were satisfied --that we were good. However, everything was not perfect; we were surrounded with the success and I just never thought things were this bad heading in the direction of a divorce.

There were many challenges I had to face to comprehend this change in my life which caused me to become very vulnerable. To go through months and months of hoping, praying and using my faith, it was hard for me to conclude that my marriage was coming to an end.

I finally learned to embrace the reality that God was in control and that while He might not change the situation in the way I wanted it to change, but if I cooperate with Him, He would change me, my character, in the situation. I've since learned that God will allow the adversity in our lives so that we might become fruitful in character and maturity.

The adversity we experience will help position us to be better prepared for what the Lord has planned for us. He knows the end before the beginning. While we are in troubling and challenging times --and although it may be uncomfortable and frustrating --it may seem like a waste of time. But only God knows what is to become of His finished work. Walking and going through troubled times have a way of causing our faith to increase; to totally trust and believe in Him. There is absolutely nothing we can do to change God's plan for our lives; however, we can decide not to cooperate with Him, which will only cause delays.

~Here's the Thing...~

It's extremely important to not allow your past to dictate your future. Just because your last employment or job didn't work out does not mean a better one won't happen in God's timing, or if you are with pain of losing a beloved or a dear friend, it does not mean we will not receive or meet new people into our circle or space who can or will become dear to us. To all things, it's a season. Satan sometimes attacks us by what is familiar or very dear to us, which causes us to become frightened, hesitant or fearful in trying or welcoming new things into your lives.

To encounter adversity is never something that is easy to embrace. When we go through trials, at the time, it never makes sense in the beginning, or the understanding of its purpose, or even the lesson of it all. When my life changed due to circumstances beyond my control it left me helpless; it left me empty and not only that, I felt unattractive, worthless, pitiful and surrounded by darkness all the time. This continued until that season was over, or complete.

If you are in a season where there is darkness all around you, *HOLD ON* because I can tell you, it will get better; it does get brighter.

Remember this:

2 Corinthians 4:17 (KJV) "For our light affliction, which is but for a moment, worketh for us a far exceeding and eternal weight of glory;"

In a Place Called There...

His Strength and His Power

When unfortunate events present themselves, life still goes on, because with the mercy of God the sun still arises, and the moon still sets come evening. People will continue their day to day responsibilities and their obligations. The bills must be paid and decisions still, must be made, and if you have a spouse and have children they still need to be supported. When a huge blow has just hit and you shake your head and you stagger a little --how do you mentally, emotionally and physically move on? How do you manage to get dress the next day and attempt to go about your normal routine as though nothing has changed, or nothing adversely has happened?

It's amazing to me that we don't realize just what lies inside of us – until we feel we have no other option, except to go into a survival mode mentality. There are a lot of people who are operating in their own strength because they feel or think they have no other options. When we operate in our own strength, we begin to deny that we are human and we start meeting the expectations of others because they don't see any abnormal-negative behaviors, so they would label that individual as a strong person. Once receiving that label there's a responsibility that goes along with it. People who present themselves as strong are typically lonely people and they have few or limited opportunities to be transparent or honest when they are around others because of this misconception.

When we allow God's power to overtake us, as the scripture tells us in 2 Corinthians 12:9-11, "But he said to me, "My grace is sufficient for you, for my power is made perfect in weakness." Therefore, I will boast all the more gladly about my weaknesses, so that Christ's power may rest on me. That is why, for Christ's sake, I delight in weaknesses, in insults, in hardships, in persecutions, in difficulties. For when I am weak, then I am strong. I have made a fool of myself, but you drove me to it. I ought to have been commended by you, for I am not in the least inferior to the "super-apostles," even though I am nothing. "In other words, those areas where we are weak, then He, God, will show Himself strong to and for us. When we operate in God's strength, we are stronger than we could ever be on our own. God's strength does not put up a front and create a stigma. Both His strength and power are like supernatural when it arises up on the inside of us. We don't need to make anything happen or meet expectations of people. With God's strength we can cry, we can yell, we can make mistakes, we can be silent, and we can even laugh. Now, when we allow God's power to strengthen us there will be some ups and some downs, until you are spiritually changed, and you will no longer have the see saw (if you will) ride experience. The demonstration of His strength and power working on the inside of us will reveal to us, as well as others that we are growing and maturing in Him.

~Here's the Thing...~

I used to get frustrated with people when they would make a comment or respond, such as, *"Once you are healed and get over this God will show Himself mightily in your life.* "So, whatever needed to be done to demonstrate that strength and power to move on, I did. But then, when certain things did bother me, going to certain places and memorable fragrances or aroma triggered a memory, I would deliberately ignore them and not make mention that it was a trigger spot for me. When practicing this, to me it seemed as though I was moving forward or moving on, but really, I was not. I was just suppressing how I really felt because I didn't want those around me to perceive me as weak or not moving on. However, through God's time and patience with me, I had to learn that healing takes time, and to walk in God's strength is a process. Once God's strength and power have totally submerged in your heart, mind and soul, being strong and whole is inevitable. Be patient with yourself; when you are weak that's when He is showing Himself strong on your, behalf.

Remember this:

2 Corinthians 12:10 (NIV) "That is why, for Christ's sake, I delight in weaknesses, in insults, in hardships, in persecutions, in difficulties. For when I am weak, then I am strong."

In a Place Called There...

All My Worship

When the human body does not release the pain or pressures from bad experiences it can cause other complications within our bodies or behaviors that are projected outwardly. Several studies have shown that stress, a broken heart, and pressures, to name a few, are the leading causes for some of these major killers of heart attacks, strokes, hypertension, diabetes and cancers.

Most circumstances are beyond our control. One of the remedies that can be done is finding ways to cope so that our spiritual, emotional and physical wellbeing won't be compromised.

Giving glory, honor and praise unto God is one of the ways we can show our gratitude toward Him and to acknowledge our need and desire for Him to work in our lives. Giving praise unto God is an outward expression that is displayed privately or publicly. Whatever is bottled up or trapped within us will eventually come out somehow. The key is using a positive outlet oppose to a negative outlet. Whenever we yell it out, pray it out, run it out, shout it out or cry it out, or exercise or jump it out, we are releasing the negative energies that are trying to suppress, oppress, or hold us down to hinder us from making any progress that God plans to do through us.

To praise God through an ordeal will help to strengthen your faith and keep your focus. Praising God not only displays your gratitude towards Him, but also, it's a declaration of your faith. Even though things currently are out of sorts, and the pain you are experiencing is so real and it just seems like it will never ease up, know that once you begin giving praises to God, your faith predicts otherwise that it will get better.

Giving praise unto God also puts flight to the enemy – the one who is trying to take advantage of your negative situation and he wants to destroy you. Right in the heart of my ordeal, I used praise as one of my weapons. The harder the enemy came, with an attempt to triumph over me and gain victory, the harder I praised God, which put him to flight.

~Here's the Thing...~

Before any adverse circumstances presented themselves, of which I believe God allowed, He knew that not only would I overcome them, but also, He knew firsthand *how* I would overcome them. What I am trying to say, is that initially when I started praising God before I was experiencing a grateful heart (like, from an intellectual or natural stance), it was because it was expected of me as a leader, for example; it was to a point that I was praising Him as if it was a daily routine or a natural habit. But then, I ventured into the spiritual realm wherein I realized that I was praising Him profoundly, like deeply from my heart. During this process I keenly became aware of His working within me, which enabled me to stand strong as a witness, that how praising and worshiping God will help to get you through the toughest times.

<u>Remember this</u>:

Jeremiah 20:13 (NIV) Sing to the Lord! Give praise to the Lord! He rescues the life of the needy from the hands of the wicked.

In a Place Called There...

Cut Above the Rest

     Things such as fabric, stone, or glass are cut into a specific shape to create an object, so when things are cut, they are generally cut on purpose and for a specific reason or need. When cutting bushes, grass, branches, or hair, it's to remove the bad growth, so that the good growth may grow better. With both examples the cutting is necessary, which is hard work and takes time. Depending on the size of the project some cutting can take hours, days, months and some can even take years before the process of cutting is complete. When someone experiences a crisis or goes through some sort of trouble, most of the time these challenges begin to reveal about their true character. Being under pressure has a funny way of bringing out the best, or worst out of people. When you are being squeezed the feeling of being in a tight spot can make it extremely unbearable to think, move or even breathe. This pressure can be so overwhelming that an individual would do just about anything to be relieved from the pressure. Going through trouble can cut or prune us where our character may develop to become better or worse. In the past when someone experienced trouble in their lives it was perceived the individual did something to warrant the pain and discomfort; this is not always the case. There are times God will allow suffering to purge us and remove anything unproductive that would hinder us from where we are going.

     Prayer is one amazing tool which can help the process. Through prayer it causes us to focus on God and listen to what He is saying about the situation. Prayer eases the pain and brings about a peace where there is confusion and helps us to guard our hearts properly by being more discerning. Prayer helps us and motivates us to learn to encourage ourselves when others don't have time or the patience to listen. Prayer builds up our self-esteem. Prayer strengthens and assures us that our love toward God is so necessary; gives supernatural guidance that will lead us away from danger or into a blessing.

~Here's the Thing...~

The cutting process is not easy. There are some things that will flourish and grow better when it's cut. Before my situation happened, I thought I had it all together, both naturally and spiritually. However, once the cutting process began, a few things about my character, the good and the bad, was revealed. The good within was highlighted and maturing, while the bad was being plucked out and destroyed. Through this process I learned quite a bit about myself, which meant I had to face some ugly truths about me. This is one of the most difficult things for any individual to do but it was well worth it.

Remember this:

John 15:2 (ESV) "Every branch in Me that does not bear fruit, He takes away; and every branch that bears fruit, He prunes it so that it may bear more fruit."

In a Place Called There...

The Turning Point

When you are experiencing a trial, try to remember that really, people don't mean any harm and they will give encouragement the best way they know how. I remember vividly the one thing that was mentioned to me over and over, again, was that I was going through this trial for somebody else. I tell you that was the last thing on my mind --helping someone else with their pain, their problems and their issues. What often happens when someone is dealing with an unfortunate event, people who are familiar with that individual or story is watching how it's being responded to.

Every day we hear tragedies all around us, especially the sadness and difficulties on the news. Once the story or news has been released, people watch to see how the story unfolds. Believe it or not, truly, it's the spectators that are cheering for you to have a positive end or outcome.

My circumstance was a little unusual or strange, if you will. I didn't realize that people who were familiar with the situation was observing me profusely, to see how I would respond. It is extremely important how you respond to a negative circumstance in your life because it will be the response that will be remembered the most.

When you are in the center of turmoil, pain and confusion, the last thing on your mind is who is watching. Even though the response to it all is energetic and spirited, here are some helpful tips to make it a little brighter:

- **_Your Choice of Company_** -- It's imperative to be among the right company during your challenges. Surround yourself with people who will celebrate you and not tolerate you. When going through your journey be careful who you travel with. Have you ever gone on a trip with someone who was miserable, complained the entire time and caused some sort of strife on the entire trip? The environment is very tense; you would just rather go home because there is no enjoyment on the trip. Being connected to the wrong people may cause you to become bitter and miserable instead of growing and maturing from the challenge.

- **_Your Conversation_** -- Dealing with a circumstance, especially when it is scandalous, people are going to talk and have their own opinions about your situation. When you are in the center of a situation and in pain because of it, you are vulnerable to listen to just about anyone in order to receive comfort, answers or looking to be justified for your own mistakes. You see, pain can cause a person to speak carelessly about things that should be kept between you and the individual involved. I remember during my situation that so much talk was going on. Some people where genuinely concerned while others were being nosey and just wanted to keep the whispering, the muttering, and the gossip going. There were many times, I realized, that I was playing right into the hands of those that wanted to keep things going, by saying too much. Through time, I learned to be quiet because I realized that discernment was taking place; before responding or commenting I would remove myself from the conversation, because my healing and my maturing was beginning to take place, I now understood. So, in the middle of your trial, guard your conversation closely.

- ***Choose Your Course*** -- Experiencing something uncomfortable is never easy to deal with. Almost always the immediate thoughts were *when will this be over; when will I stop crying; and when will my suffering end.* Giving up is an easy way out of anything. However, staying on course, especially when it looks hopeless, but you know it's a good thing, can be very challenging. One good thing I noticed about staying on course is that things would flow very well together. When one obstacle had been completed, well, then here comes another; this is all to build our spiritual muscles, to make us stronger, and to prepare us for greater. I have a tenacious spirit and I don't like to rehearse the *"what Ifs"*. From my past experiences I've learned you can never know the ending to the story unless you strive to the end. So, I held on because I wanted to see what the end would be.

~Here's the Thing...~

Now, depending on the way or how you respond, given the above information shared, could enable a favorable outcome for the rest of your life. If you handle your next challenge correctly, it can develop honor, respect and your dignity to be restored. No one is perfect and there really should be no argument with a person's character if they handle a brutal or painful challenge with class and grace.

Remember this:
1 Peter 5:10 (ESV) "And after you have suffered a little while, the God of all grace, who has called you to his eternal glory in Christ, will himself restore, confirm, strengthen, and establish you."

In a Place Called There...

Hiding in Plain Sight

When God allows others to be hidden from you, it can be perceived as an inconvenience. Without any warning or explanation God will move people out of our lives, relocate us or hinder our plans. These efforts are to protect, restore and replenish us.

To be under God's protection is similar or likened as a covering. When we are exposed and vulnerable to pain, our flaws and mistakes can be more magnified than normal. This can affect our character and influence. Sometimes when we are authentic as to who we really are, not everyone can handle it. This is one of the reasons why God may hide an individual or individuals from your environment while you are going through your challenge.

Another reason, why God might conceal others from you, is for your preparation. When we pursue a level of greatness we must be prepared. This time of preparation may involve more gaining more Godly wisdom, His strength, His power and His anointing to accomplish what we are set out or called to do.

~True Story~

It was very personal to me when the Lord instructed me to leave my home in Mechanicsburg, Pennsylvania and move back to Philadelphia. I wanted to be obedient. During this time the plot and plan of the enemy was so intense upon me; I felt he was surely out to destroy me. I was willing to stand strong and be obedient to make the move. I had a made-up mind to go through this process, no matter what happened or what I would have to do. Eventually, things became so unbearable with my life in Mechanicsburg, and I had no other choice but to leave.

Once I relocated, I was able to be around people who knew nothing about me nor my situation. This allowed me to receive the proper healing, protection and restoration.

~*Here's the Thing...*~

To be isolated is not a pleasant feeling, but at times, it is necessary. When you notice people leaving you or being distant from you suddenly, don't fret. Realize and appreciate that God is redirecting your path to take you to something better than before – to greater.

In a Place Called There...

_____
_____
_____
_____
_____
_____
_____
_____
_____
_____

It's a Pre-Mature Set-Up

One of my passed experiences was working as a catering manager with some of the most prestige's hotels such as Adams Mark Hotel, Four Points Sheraton, Holiday Inn and the Four Seasons Hotel. My primary responsibility was to book functions at one of the property sites and carry out the client's event requests. The most essential part of any client's function or event was the set-up for the event. The set-up consisted the time of the event, the place, the materials needed, the individuals involved, the theme and their purpose for the event.

These expectations of the client had to be met for them to have a "WOW" experience and a successful event. When setting up for an event in the hotel business there was always a shorter route or longer route way of getting things done. In my experience, the hotels would choose the shorter route more often than the longer route for various reasons. Usually the shorter route of the set-up was considered often for the sake of time. In the hotel business time was money because there was, usually, more than two to three events going on at the same time, but in different rooms. We noticed that when we took the shorter route mistakes were made which impacted the expectation of the client, which caused them to be displeased with the end results of our services. Needless to say, with an effort to please the clients and to display integrity, the hotel would have to either give a discount, refund money or suffer their credibility, which made it more difficult to gain more clients for future businesses.

In the same light, when our lives are orchestrated by God, we must follow His set-up which is His ultimate plan. Only the very best is prepared for us because of His love toward us. The process we go through in our lives is only a pre-mature set-up towards our destiny, and God certainly knows what He is doing to get us to that expected end. Jeremiah 29:11 (NIV) "For I know the plans I have for you," declares the Lord, "plans to prosper you and not to harm you, plans to give you hope and a future."

God will allow us to move into neighborhoods and/or He'll provide for us gainful employment so that we may obtain the necessary and required training and experiences for where we are headed, to our expected end. God will use the people we meet along the way to give us the resources we need to help us fulfill that particular purpose; He will make all things available to us in order to gain experience for where we are going.

Now, concerning God's pre-mature set-up for our lives, it's very tempting to choose the shorter route. The shorter route saves time; the shorter route decreases suffering, the shorter route is easier. What the shorter route does not provide however, is growth, maturity and wisdom. The complete experience of the process will allow us to appreciate the success even the more.

~Here's the Thing...~

We live in a world where everything is done quickly --an effort to get several things done for the sake of time. Going through a process, taking the longer route, may seem as if nothing will ever get accomplished or the goal will never be met. So, whenever you have a process consider taking the longer route; this way is always better because there is nothing like the *whole experience* of it! So, position yourself to cooperate with the Lord and avoid seeking quicker ways around your process.

Remember this:
Romans 8:28 (KJV) "And we know that all things work together for good to them that love God, to them who are the called according to his purpose."

In a Place Called There...

The Vantage Point

With every trip, circumstance, entertainment or whatever someone is involved in, there are different perspectives. To have different perspectives things may come to a surface that was never noticed before. When a group of people come together to strategize for a meeting it's great to have different perspectives. This will reduce stress, confusion, having a sense of order, and prevents embarrassment and any unnecessary pain and suffering.

The vantage point is when and how a person has the advantage for the perspective. This gives a person a more detailed outlook than the average viewers. There are some instances from where a person stands or what they know or what was revealed to them, which gives a different perspective of the circumstance from everyone else.

God is a restorer and He delights to prove Himself strong in our lives. What we see and what we know can sometimes be both conflicting and confusing. We can see a horrible situation, see the suffering, even see things caving in, but what do we know.

When you are in the middle of your circumstance, find the strength to stand on what was spoken to you by God and hold onto that revelation –that spoken word. When someone experiences one hit after the other, the knowing that they will have is this too will pass; things will get better and this affliction is only but for a moment. This is what helps a person to stand and not give up. So, I ask you, what is your perspective on your circumstance?

~Here's the Thing...~

What I learned over the years is to focus on what I know and to operate from my vantage point. People generally react to the reality of their circumstance. If you know you shall live and not die --stand, live and breathe from that vantage point. Do not deviate from what you know. If you know you are the head and not the tail, keep your head up, be resilient and have a robust walk from that vantage point, and none other.

In a Place Called There...

_____
_____
_____
_____
_____
_____
_____
_____
_____
_____

Swallow the Pill and Keep it Moving

Most people do not like taking medications in the form of pills, especially if they must take them several times a day. There is always some reason why taking a pill is necessary --a requirement for some reason or another by the doctors, if you will and the results will be noticed if they are taking them or not.

Tragedies are certainly unpleasant and devastating. Life challenges will show up in our lives from time to time –this we know is inevitable. Once unfortunate circumstances occur, there will be things revealed concerning ourselves, and others; e.g., who forgave and who did not; dysfunctionalities from a child that were never corrected, or who are your true friends and who are not, just to name a few.

There are a number of revelations that are difficult to face during trouble. When we are faced with a difficult trial that is overwhelming and heart wrenching, people may have tendencies to turn to negative resources. Negative resources such as, displaying violent tendencies, usage of substance abuse or allowing their lives to head in a destructive direction.

When a person is in pain, they can easily become selfish. They are only focused on the pain and they will likely do anything to be relieved from their discomfort. Pain blinds us to have the lack of understanding, to realize that unpleasant things happen to give us an opportunity to reach and pursue for better.

One form of pill to swallow is in the area of *blame,* which is usually the first thing people do when something bad occurs. When placing blame somewhere and/or on someone, it gives an explanation and some comfort as to what transpired, whether it's true or false. When we place blame on others, we are quick to take the spotlight or focus off ourselves. Most people like to have an explanation or a justification as to what took place. No one is perfect and looking back, we all can see and later realize that things could have been handled or done differently. Instead of pushing blame, accept the error, forgive yourself, receive the lesson and move on. There is better.

~*True Story*~

The route or plan I initially had to cope with my situation was to go on road trips and consistently turn toward my faith. During those road trips gave me the opportunity to think clearer, talk it out, pray it out or cry it out. There were so many revelations I learned about myself, both good and bad. These revelations were both painful and humbling, all at the same time because I had to look at me and no one else. While going through this process I embraced the fact that I was not perfect and that I can hurt and disappoint people. I finally realized that I do not have to be accommodating for people to like and accept me. I now understand how to love and respect myself and not put that responsibility on others. I now can say no and be okay with the consequences of that decision. I no longer lose sleep from worrying about what others may say or think about me. I accept that I can make mistakes, forgive myself and move on.

~*Here's the Thing...*~

When faced with something difficult and overwhelming never allow your painful experience to take you to the extreme. Search for positive coping skills or aids.

When bad things happen in the middle of your pain, practice these things:

- Give a word of encouragement

- Help someone else who may be hurting

Great blessings can come out of your tragedy and cause you to triumph in God's time.

Remember this:

Proverbs 28:13 (ESV) "Whoever conceals his transgressions will not prosper but he who confesses and forsakes them will obtain mercy."

In a Place Called There…

_____
_____
_____
_____
_____
_____
_____
_____
_____

It Only Takes One Bite

When you start believing what the enemy presents to you, this belief will start spreading like poisonous venom from a snake bite. If you are ever bitten by some snakes you might see symptoms of redness, swelling, tingling of the limbs, sweating and severe pain; you might even experience some vomiting and/or sight problems.

A snake bite may become fatal over time if it's not treated promptly. Once the venom is released it then goes through the lymphatic body system causing side effects, such as bleeding, kidney failure, breathing problems and tissue death around the bite which may result in a loss of a limb. These effects are from one bite.

Venom in many snakes affects every organ system in the human body and the venom releases toxins such i.e., cytotoxins, hemotoxins, neurotoxins and mycotoxins, which can cause a large vast of symptoms. The strength of each snake's venom differs, so the severity is dependent upon which type of snake. Some snake bites are not life threatening depending on the age and the health of its victim. The facts are comparable to our spirituality. The venom of the enemy operates the same but from a natural standpoint.

Although the enemy is not in a rush to destroy us, however, eventually, that is his goal. The seeds that are planted are strategically planted with a purpose to set up in the direction of destruction, which is why it's so important to let things go; to constantly pray about everything and seek what

God is saying in every unfortunate circumstance. The attacks of the enemy may not impact everyone the same. One bite may be fatal to an individual where it's a spiritual life or death situation as oppose to someone else who may just need ongoing treatment. This depends on the spiritual maturity of that individual. The enemy's goal is to keep us from accomplishing and receiving anything from God, and to eventually destroy us.

There are remedies and medications to heal a person from a snake bite such as, IV fluid, stretchy bandages for support and ongoing medications. Spiritually, there are remedies to overcome a bite as well. Some ways are reading God's Word consistently continually; surround yourself with people whose focus is on God; live according to His Word, prayer with fasting; continuous fellowshipping and communing with God. When practicing these things, it will lessen our chances of getting bitten, or if we do, the healing process can take affect faster with less damage to repair.

~True Story~

During the midst of my trial, I felt so vulnerable. Everything was out in the open and my life became an open book. This exposure revealed my strengths and my weaknesses. It's funny how the enemy magnifies our weaknesses so that we won't or can't t operate in our strengths. The enemy bit me; the venom of guilt, shame and accusation started to affect me spiritually. Staying on the routine of my treatment plan was vital. I had to stay prayed up, keep my head in the Word of God and worship like I never worshipped before. Keeping this routine has helped me tremendously to get back to a good and healthy wellbeing and spiritual health.

~Here's the Thing...~

One of the most difficult things to wrap your mind around is something you didn't expect to happen. You just were not prepared physically nor mentally for it. It's during this time the enemy evaluates our most vulnerable areas and goes for the attack.

Remember this:

John 10:10 (KJV) "The thief cometh not, but for to steal, and to kill, and to destroy: I am come that they might have life, and that they might have it more abundantly."

In a Place Called There...

_____
_____
_____
_____
_____
_____
_____
_____
_____
_____
_____
_____
_____
_____
_____
_____
_____
_____
_____

Not Bitter - Just Better

Bitterness is produced from the root. Bitterness is like weeds that grow in a garden to hinder the garden from becoming healthy; eventually the weeds will kill the good growth. There are different methods that can be used to remove weeds. This depends on the depth of the root. The less complicated weeds --young weeds before they establish root, can simply be pulled up. There are some weeds that require digging to get to the root system. The most difficult weeds to remove are the ones that had a length of time to grow, thereby establishing extensive roots.

To treat this condition and maintain a good and healthy appearance, a series of pulling up the weeds and utilizing chemicals with consistency, until the roots are destroyed. The heart is the platform of the body and soul. Without the heart it is difficult to love and display that love with true affection; it is difficult to be motivated or have any compassion. The heart is so vital; it is mentioned 830 times in the Bible --King James' Version.

When we experience something that angers, disappoints or pains us in some way, the longer we allow it to marinate in our hearts and greater the chance that those feelings will establish a root system. Deal with the issues while it's fresh and the weeds are young and can be pulled up from our hearts with humility and prayer. If the root of bitterness has become stronger, using the Word of God, prayer and some fasting may be required. This is necessary because the root has grown a little deeper and now there may have to be some digging to get to the root and destroy the unwanted feeling. If the root system has already developed and it is extensive, this may require a professional to help sort out the root of the problem or the bitterness may lead to death of an individual's spirit where the experience of true freedom from feeling angry and miserable may never become a reality.

~True Story~

It took me years to get to the point when I didn't feel a lump in my throat and swelled up in tears feeling overwhelmed each time I had to speak with my ex-spouse or see him. Over the years I had to consistently work on not allowing anger, disappointment and hurt to overtake me. I had made up my mind that I was not going to be miserable for the rest of my life –to never experience total freedom again. The Lord is our gardener and He is the expert in landscaping of our hearts.

~Here's the Thing...~

One of the worst things we can do is not be honest and hide behind how we really feel. In the scripture Jeremiah 17:9 (ASV) says "The heart is deceitful above all things, and it is exceedingly corrupt: who can know it?" Only God can search the heart and He alone knows how to deal with and destroy the things that hinders us from the peaceful, prosperous blessed life He has for us.

Here are a few suggestions I found helpful, to me, which helped to keep bitterness out and in turn I incurred a good root system.

- Submerge in God's Word and live your life.

- Pray without ceasing.

- Love, even when you don't want to love back.

- Have compassion, even when it's not fair.

Remember this:

Proverbs 4:23 (KJV) "Keep thy heart with all diligence; for out of it are the issues of life."

In a Place Called There...

The Monkey Bar Syndrome

People have their own definition and experience concerning forgiveness. One consistent viewpoint that I have heard many people say and agree with is that to forgive someone is not for the other person, but for ourselves. Depending on the level of the offence it can be difficult to forgive immediately. Some hurts are deep where it can affect our attitude and behavior towards others. I once read a quote on social media that stated, "If you never heal from what hurt you, you will bleed on people who never cut you". If the offense is not addressed and confronted, over time, this will lead to bitterness and resentment.

Forgiveness can be tricky. The moment you think you forgave someone and move forward, here comes along a person, place or thing that triggers a tender spot that reminds you of the hurt and you begin to go in a circle of anger, bitterness and resentment all over again.

When an offense occurs one of the first things a person should do is search within themselves to make sure it could have been avoided. To search within ourselves will allow us to take note to determine if it could have been avoided. Sometimes we can cause an offense when we say something we didn't mean or may have been misunderstood. Then, there are times we do absolutely nothing to warrant an offense. Forgiveness is a choice; we can decide to truly forgive or not. There are quite a few people who feel no matter how sincerely sorry a person may be for the offense they still feel there should be a punishment to be given. If we do not forgive and let go of the pain and the hurt from the offense, we are the ones, in the long run, who will suffer for it. Who wants to walk around all day in pain, mad at the world and just miserable --all because of being hurt, while the one who offended us is free of pain, joyful and moved on with their lives?

Part of being human is having a memory which is given to us by God. We are going to have memories of good things and bad things, as well as when they happened, the time and the day. One of the things that was taught to me while growing up in church was in order to forgive you must forget the offense supported with the scripture found in Matthew 6:14 (ESV) "For if you forgive others their trespasses, your heavenly Father will also forgive you…"How do you forget and act like something never happened, especially if it was traumatic? The truth is you will always remember the offense but in order to be forgiven we must forgive the offender. The proof that the offender has not been forgiven is when we keep rehearsing it and we continue to be angry again and again; we keep talking about the situation year after year; we keep crying over it with no peace in sight. When situations occur that reminds us of the offense, think of it as a test or a measuring stick to reveal or show you your growth or your improvement. This is how you can tell if you have truly let go and moved on.

To forgive and forget doesn't mean to ignore the incident as though it never happened. It takes humility, courage and strength to communicate and not hold anything against the offender. This does not mean you have to be the best of friends, or that you must talk to each other every day or continue where you left off. No, there are times the offense will change the dynamic of the relationship. To forgive is a risk of being vulnerable but it is crucial to move forward and be free.

~*True Story*~

Anytime someone would ask me questions regarding what happened with my marriage or what's going on they would get an earful from me. If you were willing to listen to me, I would talk. It was brought to my attention one day that I wasn't really over the incident and I hadn't let go and assuredly, I had not forgiven. In my tone of voice, you could still hear the hurt, the lengthy explanations to justify my rights while tears streamed down my face.

Those were insightful clues that I wasn't completely over the hurt at all. I remember feeling, that if I truly forgave, it meant that I was giving up my *victim's* rights.

It was easy for me to point the finger, be angry, to be filled with pain and hurt from being betrayed. What I didn't realize was that holding on to these justified feelings were affecting my current and new relationships that were on the horizon. I began to bleed over people who never cut me, but I was taking the hurts of the past: anger, rejections and betrayals into new relationships.

~Here's the Thing...~

There is so much that is taught, preached and even written on the power of forgiveness, but until you truly walk in forgiveness, that's when it becomes real. This devotional book couldn't even be published and provided until I reached a place in forgiveness that allowed me to see my part of the offence and asked the offender to forgive me. That is true forgiveness, true growth and moving forward.

Remember this:

Ephesians 4:31-32 (KJV) "Let all bitterness, and wrath, and anger, and clamour, and evil speaking, be put away from you, with all malice: And be ye kind one to another, tenderhearted, forgiving one another, even as God for Christ's sake hath forgiven you."

In a Place Called There...

The Pause Button

On most equipment you can find a pause button that will have choices like forward, back or rewind buttons. The pause button was created to temporarily stop so that we can attend to something else for just a moment or two without starting over. This button is commonly used when interrupted while watching a movie, listening to a recorded show or tuned into an inspirational message. Instead of starting over pursuant to the distraction, you can just hit the pause button.

Our lives can be so fast paced that we forget to notice what is going on around us. For this reason, many people have developed an impulsive behavior due to not taking their time or from making hasty decisions. This is because of the constant race against time. To be impulsive can be negative or positive. On the positive side being impulsive can prevent procrastination. On the negative side being impulsive can cause careless decision making, e.g., not thinking things through; financial hardships due to impulsive buying; and health issues relating to stress, and so on. The pause button is located within our minds. Going through one difficulty after another can be so overwhelming. One of the most therapeutic methods is taking a break from it all. Create a pause button strategy that works for you. For some it may be a quiet walk in the park listening to the wind moving softly through the trees, and for others it may be sitting on the beach observing the waves bouncing on the shore with the warmth of the sun beaming on your skin. And then some may find a road trip to do wonders in giving them time to think and to take inventory and evaluate themselves.

~True Story~

After going through a brutal illness like breast cancer and then right after that a heart-breaking divorce, and then, to see and experience a season of peace was not even a thought. In order to maintain any sanity, I often would take road trips or go to the beach to listen to the waves. This method was not only relaxing for me, which was my pause button, but also this is where I found most my closeness to God -- my secret place.

~Here's the Thing...~

When you go through something so harsh you may need more than professional help. Find what works for you and take a break; find where your pause button is located and take advantage of it --use it.

Remember this:

Philippians 4:6 (KJV) "Be careful for nothing; but in everything by prayer and supplication with thanksgiving let your requests be made known unto God."

In a Place Called There...

_____
_____
_____
_____
_____
_____
_____
_____
_____

It's Not Easy Being You

It's wonderful, in fact, it's amazing how God gives each of us different gifts and talents. The gifts and talents may be in the same category but the way He enables you to display or present them can bring freshness and something totally different. Some restaurants, hotels and clothing chains have the same mentality. They may be owned by the same company but what makes them unique and different is the style, according to that specific location. They may offer different tastes, according to the desires of the customers. You are who you are. No one knows what it takes for you to do what you do best.

~True Story~

As a child the Thanksgiving Holiday was my favorite holiday, not only because it brought our family together but because of the variety of foods that were prepared. Every year we would place a spread of food which included at least two apple pies or four sweet potato pies. Each pie was made by a different family member and the taste and texture of the pies were all slightly different. I remember preferring a piece of a particular apple pie that one aunt baked because of the crust. There was absolutely nothing wrong with the other pies; it was just the way the crust was prepared by her, which I enjoyed better.

No one knows what it takes for you to do what you do best. Only you know the level of suffering; hardship; physical discomfort; uneasiness; the anxiety; the cost; being rejected; and/or being an outcast, which developed you to be who you are.

Through the years I had to re-learn and realize my worth and walk, talk, hold my head up high as the child of the King. At one of my places of employment I had a supervisor who would often say to me "It's not easy being you." Each one of us are made perfectly by the hand of God and the world needs to see us for who we really are and not who we think we should be.

~Here's the Thing...~

No one enjoys feeling like an outcast. Some people will change their style, behavior or compromise their morals just to be accepted. One of the most powerful statements you can make in life is being who you are. If your gifts, talents and personality were not needed God would not have created you. Here are just a few tips to stay in the boundaries of who you are.

1. Don't settle: Being sick with cancer made me realize that I had only one life to live. There were goals to be reached, places I never traveled to and things that needed to be done if I desired to leave a legacy behind. We must stay focused on the things God has appointed for us to do and know that you have been anointed to do them.

2. Be confident as to who you are: What may matter to you may not matter to others. This is what makes us all different and unique. Show yourself strong in who you are, even if it looks like you are the only one who feels and sees things differently.

3. Learn to love and appreciate yourself: Believe it or not, everyone admires and is influenced by someone. Learn to admire and be influenced by yourself. True, nobody is perfect but embrace who you are and what is perfect.

4. Surround yourself with people who celebrate you --not tolerate you: Stay away from negative people. Some people are just assigned to you by the enemy to steal and suck the life out of you.

Remember this:

Psalm 138:8 (NKJV) "The Lord will perfect that which concerns me; Your mercy, O Lord, endures forever; Do not forsake the works of Your hands."

In a Place Called There...

_____
_____
_____
_____
_____
_____
_____
_____
_____

Know Your Worth

The value of some items is often ignored and taken for granted, until these items are gone. People purchase items such as jewelry, cars, houses and paintings today because of the beauty, not so much their value. When you value something, you handle it with extreme care and guarded well. In jewelry stores, car lots, houses and art galleries the owners will invest in a sophisticated alarm system and motion detectors to keep the thieves away.

Each of us has been created differently. When a woman is pregnant with twin babies, the two infants may share the same womb and have similarities, but rest assured, there will be some differences. One of the areas the enemy attacks us is when we question ourselves --*if we are good enough*? This question is usually motivated by a rejection of some kind we might have experienced. Experiencing rejection can come from many sources. The most common type of rejections that could motivate this questioning is being rejected from a relationship or marriage where you are told they no longer want to be with you; not being selected for a job you are qualified for or being rejected from friends and family members that had you around only for their convenience. None of these circumstances feel great and it can be detrimental to one's self-esteem. God created man/woman in His own image –in His likeness, so He knows us better than we know ourselves and He has placed His value within each one of us, for a specific plan and specific purpose. Unfortunately, at times, we do not realize it; we are the ones who need to be informed that we are special to God, He does have a plan, He loves us unconditionally and we must believe it.

~Here's the Thing...~

When your character is under attack because the exposure of some truths, lies and misunderstandings it's very difficult to feel as if you are worth anything at all. What was accomplished and any success before a negative circumstance presented itself seems to go out the window and forgotten. It's interesting how we evaluate and place emphasis on the word *value* today. Just because you made a mistake, got caught up in a situation, or you find yourself alone suddenly, does not mean there is no worth in you. Our value begins when we were created by God and we become more value with time. Life experiences and time allows us to learn from our lessons, so that we may mature and grow for the master's use. As you are reading this devotional, you may be in a place feeling there is no use, and you may feel all hope is lost and everything is ruin. Two things for sure, and one thing for certain, I know God is a God of second, third and fourth chances.

In a Place Called There...

_____
_____
_____
_____
_____
_____
_____
_____
_____
_____

Vessel of Honor

When we look at vessels (containers, pots, pitchers, etc.), they come in different sizes, colors and shapes to hold a certain capacity of substance based on the allotted space. They generally have a specific purpose for use when needed.

A vessel, whether it's a vase, container, jar, cup, glass, the item holds something and it's no use when it's empty. The purpose of the object, or vessel, is to fill it up with something so that it can be emptied or poured out; to be repeated over and over.

We hold up our vessels; (the heart, the soul, the mind) we can only be helpful if there's something in there of specific purpose for a specific use to pour out. Once it's poured out it must be replenished; it must be refreshed, thereby with prayer, God's Word, and some good old fashion rest. Then we are ready to pour out all over again.

Our characters as women are nurturers; we like to help. There is nothing wrong with helping but if we ourselves, are empty and have nothing to offer, we end up doing more damaged than good. Only give what you have. If you are low in resources or whatever the requirement or the need for the help, maybe, sit this one out and do what is necessary to become replenished and refreshed again.

~True Story~

My personality has always been to help others where and when I can. Whatever resource I had, be it money, knowledge, connection, or even prayer, if someone needed it, I didn't have a problem with helping and giving it.

To have such a helpful heart is a great thing but it can also be grievous when you don't have anything to give. Over the years I came to learn and understand it's not possible for me to help anyone until I help myself. I can't give nothing that I don't have. Someone deposited some good old fashion wisdom into me and told me, give what you don't need back. If you need it back, you never had it to give.

~Here's the Thing...~

Some people are helpful, however, not necessarily because of their heart but for different motives. Some people like to feel needed; some like to feel in control over someone else. We must have a pure, honest heart with the motive of simply desiring --wanting to be a blessing. The Lord won't leave us on empty. He will fill us with His amazing love, His presence and His power. Let the oil flow which will never run dry.

In a Place Called There...

_____
_____
_____
_____
_____
_____
_____
_____
_____
_____

R.E.S.P.E.C.T. Yourself

As children we are taught to respect our elders. We know not to talk back, ignore, call them names or talk at them because they were our elders. Even when some of our elders would provoke us, we knew just to walk away to avoid disrespecting them.

People are taught either at home, school or place of employment to respect their elders, but you don't hear too often about respecting ourselves. To have self-respect is realizing who you are and what you have to offer. Having self-respect is not being arrogant but its setting boundaries not to be mistreated, get in touch with who you really are, forgiving yourself for mistakes made, forgiving others and surrounding yourself with positive people.

We cannot control the opinion that other people may have toward us, however, we can control how they treat us. Some time ago, I heard this bit of wisdom and advice: "You cannot keep birds from flying over your head, but you can keep them from building a nest in your hair." --Martin Luther

Learning to respect one-self is a matter of having a clear understanding of who you are, why you are here and where you are going. There is a purpose and destiny for everyone. We must love ourselves, be respectful to ourselves, and we must be patient with ourselves enough to get there; to that place called there or our destiny, designed by God.

~True Story~

Learning to respect myself was something new for me to embrace during this trial. I would accommodate others, despite how I felt, to avoid them from feeling awkward while around me. One evening the Holy Spirit spoke to me about me and He whispered gently to me, "Learn how to respect your feelings, and teach others to do the same. Stop accommodating others, despite how they feel. If it hurts, then it hurts, if it's uncomfortable, then it's uncomfortable, if I don't agree, then I don't agree".

While growing up the friends I made in school or met from the neighborhood were a privilege to me, so having friends was always of great value to me. My failures and successes were always determined by who I was around. I never thought I was perfect, but I felt that I had to be perfect because I was the oldest and the pacesetter of the family. Things were expected of me that were not yet fulfilled by my other siblings, so I decided to go a different route. Instead of being the first to go to college I decided to be a full-time employee. Instead of being grateful for my job and pursuing other opportunities I began complaining; I left the job and everyone else around me were complaining and left the job as well.

~Here's the Thing...~

There are many people who settle for less than what their capabilities are, and they do so for a variety of reasons. There is nothing wrong with learning from others and applying what you learned to your lifestyle. Learn to set your own standards for yourself; build and stay focus as you grow. I was greatly influenced by the friends I made in school, the neighborhood I lived in, the crew I hung around, the co-workers I worked with and the church groups I worshipped with. Instead of following the path for my life I allowed distractions from others to overtake me and move me off course. I repeat, there is absolutely nothing wrong with learning from others and applying what you learned and grasped to your life, however, don't abort the total plan God has for your life.

In a Place Called There...

Inner Healing Brings a Fresh Focus

Having a surgical procedure can be very nerve racking. Whether it is a short or lengthy procedure, going under local or general anesthesia –and wherein cutting is involved, this prompts a healing process. Depending on the type of surgery there is a timeline of how the area should look when it's healed.

Surgeries are recommended when something within the body needs to be repaired or corrected to prevent continued harm and hinders growth in the rest of the body. Once the surgery has been completed and the healing process has begun, the medical professional will keep the patient under watch to make sure the blood is flowing correctly.

After a surgery, the common risk a patient may suffer are blood clots, which may cause other complications or even death. Inner healing operates in a similar way. When we have both a seen and unforeseen, and unfortunate circumstance, God will use that as an opportunity to perform surgery on us. Whatever the incident, some sort of damage took place that needs to be repaired or corrected. While our hearts are open, hurt and vulnerable things will be revealed about ourselves, this is part of the healing process. Once the healing begins, natural surgery complications can occur, such as a blood clot. This type of clot prevents the blood of Jesus from flowing properly and can cause complications concerning our prayer life, for example, neglecting ourselves from God's Word; isolating ourselves from people who are assigned to encourage us.

With surgeries you may still encounter issues along the way such as soreness, swelling and tenderness; this will become less annoying with time. There are levels of healing and an individual should keep in mind to be patient with their healing.

Fresh Focus begins with a new perspective after being healed from an unfortunate circumstance. While the healing process is still taking place after the incident, you may still have issues, such as feeling tenderness --the soreness from the memory. You may experience some swelling at times, where you thought you were over it, but something occurred to expand the pain once more. But when we are nicely and completely healed, those issues are no longer a concern.

~True Story~

My having to walk through the experience of a failed marriage and facing the scandal on a Christian leadership level was humiliating and painful. In addition to dealing with the level of trial and all that was involved, I also had to deal with the truth about myself. While I was cut, broken into pieces, bleeding out and in constant excruciating pain, herein is where God took that opportunity to do surgery within my heart. He repaired and corrected my character, changed my perspective on life, gave me wisdom, increased discernment within myself and I was able to get some rest.

~Here's the Thing...~

When you are walking in pain, please, don't avoid the opportunity to see any issues or flaws that are revealed to you. This is just God's way of taking the opportunity to repair, mold, shape, and correct you so that your perspective can be fresh.

Remember this:
Psalm 51:17 (ESV) "The sacrifices of God are a broken spirit; a broken and a contrite heart, O God, you will not despise."

In a Place Called There…

The Beauty of Waiting

When you are faced with a choice as to whether you should wait or not, it is a wonderful feeling to see a favorable outcome because you waited. One example of waiting could be with the DMV or in an emergency room. This type of waiting can be long and tedious, but you could use that time to get other things accomplished. When I need to take a trip to the DMV or the emergency room, I knew there would be a lengthy wait. In preparation of the pending wait I would bring a bag along with me. Inside the bag I would bring bills, correspondence to review, materials to read, church lessons –the things I needed to catch up on while waiting. Waiting for me, sometimes, was a good thing and an opportunity I used to get something else accomplished because of my constantly being on the move. As my service number was drawing closer, I would put away my work so that I would be ready to immediately get up because my number was about to be called.

Waiting does not last forever. You do get the turn to be next in obtaining the promises God has for you. While waiting, you should not be idled, just watching the time go by, but you should be occupying yourself, constructively, while you are waiting. There are moments in our lives where we must be still because sometimes it's difficult to pinpoint a moving target. When we are moving there is no time to evaluate our motives and get a better understanding as to who we are and where we are going. However, when we are still, we can take a look at our attitude to see if we have the right or wrong perspective concerning our lives. We can also improve and shape our character while it's being built.

~True Story~

Working for the Lord has always been my joy, however there were things I took upon myself, and God had nothing to do with it. Although it was still for the benefit of God's kingdom, it wasn't what He had instructed me to do. This caused me to become frustrated, bitter, feeling neglected, abandoned; in fact, this caused me to be unhappy with life in general. While on this unfortunate journey this caused me to be removed from all church leadership responsibilities, and I had an opportunity to sit and wait. It was hard, but it was well worth it.

~Here's the Thing...~

When you are constantly busy and relentlessly on the go, it is difficult to see potential problems and then accept the responsibility of how you could avoid unnecessary pain if you were not so busy. Even though what you are doing may not be entirely wrong, the motive behind it may be wrong. This can only be observed truthfully and honestly when an individual is still given the opportunity to look things over and realize what could have been done differently.

Remember this:

Psalm 37:34 (KJV) "Wait on the Lord, and keep his way, and he shall exalt thee to inherit the land: when the wicked are cut off, thou shalt see it."

In a Place Called There…

Waiting to be Blessed

The world we live in now is so fast paced, with a right now mentality; nobody likes to wait for anything. In most cases, in order to receive something, some amount of waiting is involved; this is a given fact. In department stores, especially during Black Friday around the holiday season, you can find some real good deals. The most annoying part of shopping is standing in long lines to purchase your item. Depending on the product the wait line can be over an hour. Some people will camp out to have a better chance to get the product. Their wait is longer, of course, because it's overnight, but their chances are greater to obtain the prize. Waiting in long lines can make an individual weary and you may begin to feel weak. I remember having an experience waiting in a long line and feeling dizzy and faint.

Sometimes I would fight through this weak feeling and the dizziness and I would remain in line. Then there were other times I would succumb to how I felt, and I would get out of the line to get myself together. Once I start feeling better or obtained a drink of water, etc. I would either start at the beginning of the line or I just decided to forfeit my purchase or the reason I was standing in the line.

There is something special, however, about waiting on the Lord. Waiting will allow us to see some unbelievable outcomes. Although waiting on God can be a good thing, it becomes tire some to some, because they can only see the beginning of a thing or the situation. There is nothing to measure or compare just to see how much longer it will take before your prayer is answered or that you have finally arrived. While you are waiting you may get weak, feel dizzy, faint and become weary. It's the enemy's job to make sure we believe that our promises will never come to pass. So, if we are waiting in a line, he creates a delusion for us to think that we are to get out of line, lose our spot, get ourselves together would be the best thing to do. If you stick with it, stay in line despite how you feel, pray yourself through it while moving closer to the reward, you will surely obtain it.

~Here's the Thing...~

Waiting is not an easy thing to do, especially when you know there is something great to obtain while you wait. I'm a very impatient person and anxiety is one of my weak points. Being put in a position where there is nothing you can do but wait and trust God for the outcome is a humbling experience. The best thing I could have done, faced with my circumstances, was doing it God's way. There were many times of weariness, feeling faint, wanting to get out line so to speak and get myself together and do things my own way. I'm always intrigued by how a successful person got there. Usually, when you hear the person's story, there was some sort of challenge or struggle. One thing that is very important and made perfectly clear to me was time. If I get out of line the choice was to start over again or forfeit the opportunity of receiving His promise to me all together. It has all been worth the wait --to stay right in line and He keeps the line moving.

Remember this:

Isaiah 40:31 (KJV) "But they that wait upon the Lord shall renew their strength; they shall mount up with wings as eagles; they shall run, and not be weary; and they shall walk, and not faint."

In a Place Called There…

Hurry Up and Wait

When I was diagnosed with breast cancer in 2007, I was waiting to get prepped for surgery. One of the most interesting things the nurse said to me was that *"we have to hurry up and wait"*. I didn't understand the logic to hurry up and wait.

When people are scheduled for surgery, usually there are quite a few procedures going on all at once. In the medical field there is no guarantee that a patient won't experience a complication during the surgery or a procedure. Even though there is a possibility of complications, this does not mean the next scheduled person shouldn't get prepared for their surgery in order to avoid delays.

When we receive a word from God that He will bless us, usually this won't happen overnight. There is a preparation season that must be endured first before we can be trusted and qualified with what God has for us. During the preparation season there are moments where things will get tough and lonely.

There are some things that will happen to you that will seem unfair; for example, people that you thought you could trust will turn against you; you may be lied on or misunderstood, just to name a few, but know, this is all part of the process. It's in the preparation and waiting season that will reflect who we really are because our character is being built. Each of these things are done in God's timing because He knows the work that needs to be done in each of us to obtain what He has for us.

~True Story~

During my season of struggle, I learned quickly that I can't prepare myself for something I can't see. I would try to fix myself by not yelling and getting so extremely angry; I would listen more before speaking; I would control my emotions to not be so vulnerable and needy. These were good things to focus on in order to become better, but I still needed to depend on God to handle these things on the inside of me and put them in order so that I could become effective. The rebukes and corrections were not easy, but God allowed me to experience certain things to complete me. It was my responsibility to cooperate with God so that I could receive all He had for me.

Remember this:

Psalm 138:8 (KJV) "The Lord will perfect that which concerneth me: thy mercy, O Lord, endureth forever: forsake not the works of thine own hands."

In a Place Called There…

_____
_____
_____
_____
_____
_____
_____
_____
_____
_____

The Power of Obedience While Waiting

The word obedience is not a cliché that is used for religious purposes only, but it is a hopeful race towards God's promises. In order to obey God, we must understand what He commands. God is not required to explain and give details when He directs us to do something.

We can easily misinterpret what God is saying. We can hear His Word and miss the meaning; we can see the signs and miss the significance. The true knowledge of God is born out of obedience to Him and it is for those who follow Christ. Our position is to accept the Word of God by faith and then obey it. Today we live in a world where everyone likes to justify and present their case why they didn't fully obey a specific direction.

True obedience does not procrastinate, justify or prolong the instruction by asking questions. We can delay our own blessing by operating in disobedience. It's our duty to obey God's command; its His duty to keep His promises once we obey.

Obedience is a process and the conditioning of one's heart to accept and carry out the full command of the Lord and that obedience will be tested. Each test that is passed involves a new level of obedience to follow. Depending on the magnitude of the test, the reward is matched or higher. When graduating from high school or college every student that passed received a diploma or degree, appropriately. There will be some students who get special recognition because of the extra effort they took and made before graduating. They went to the next level to obtain a higher prize. To pursue obedience is a choice one makes that is not easy because the choice is personal --not public. However, the reward of obedience is publicly displayed; everyone can see publicly the cost that was involved as to how that person became so blessed.

~True Story~

While going through the divorce I felt so much pain, confusion, hurt and betrayal. I heard in a message some time ago that going through a divorce is almost the likeness of death. After time went by, it was clear to me that it was important and purposeful for me to *not* move away because I needed to re-build my creditability the enemy was trying to destroy. The Lord knew I would eventually be healed completely, so I later understood that there were many reasons and purposes for all that I had to go through.

Things were very intense because I was being tested of how I would react. Normally, under extreme pressure --especially females --the reaction would come from a place of pain and it is not quiet nor a pretty sight, but I was expected and encouraged to do so. Any one of those reactions people could understand and relate to because of the circumstance.

During this time my obedience was extremely important because God wanted to show me off. If I reacted according to the expectation of people, God wouldn't get the glory, and the enemy would have been proven to be right. I would have regrets that would affect me and my children for the rest of our lives. Initially at that time, I could not understand why I couldn't move away as soon as I wanted to so that I could be quiet and not have to defend myself all the time. It just didn't make sense until 10 years later; now, I can hold my head up with no regrets. I was tested and God knew this situation would only launch me to my knees harder.

~Here's the Thing...~

Obedience is not easy, nor does it come naturally. There is a personal struggle and sacrifice when dealing with obedience. But when God gives instructions a stronger purpose is behind it and His ways are not our ways. When God sets things up it's not only for that moment, or for the time you are going through your challenge, but He gives sweet victory 10 years and beyond.

Remember this:

1 Samuel 15:22 (KJV) "And Samuel said, Hath the LORD as great delight in burnt offerings and sacrifices, as in obeying the voice of the LORD? Behold, to obey is better than sacrifice, and to hearken than the fat of rams."

In a Place Called There...

_____
_____
_____
_____
_____
_____
_____
_____
_____
_____

Pending Status

During this season ladies you may have to check up on it! Let me explain. The best example I can give is purchasing an item from a catalog. When purchasing an item from a catalog you must use a credit or debit card; you purchase the item and you wait for a confirmation number. Now, your item has been approved for purchase. Usually there is information that the order will take up to 2-3 weeks, from the time ordered, shipped, and its arrival to you. After the order is placed, the company will provide a link or status of your item so that you can conveniently check from time to time pending the delivery or arrival to you. So, after you purchase, you patiently wait for it. When checking the status at times it may say *still processing* or *pending* or the status may say shipped for delivery. When we stand on God's Word, and we believe and we have faith in Him, He will allow us to go through the process so we may be eligible to receive the blessing. Herein we are not eligible or qualified, so that eventually we will receive the blessing.

You see, to pay the price for something enables us to become eligible or qualified to receive it after we measured up the cost. There are some spiritual blessings and levels that will make us qualified. When we are finished paying for the item, it's now time for the processing status. The processing status can be quick, or it may take some time. It just depends on the order – i.e., if the item is in stock or if everything, like the requested information is complete to process. When we have faith in God, we already know it's done in the spirit realm; now it's time to wait for the manifestation of what was promised. It can be annoying or discouraging to periodically check on something and find the status to be still pending or processing, but at the same time it would be encouraging to know that the order was not denied, but it is on the way.

The assurance of receiving something is that you paid for it. Only you can cancel the order, and in most cases, it may not be refundable, however you may receive credit for your purpose. What you may get back on credit may not be the original product, but you may have to choose something that is second best. Why pay for something so costly and change your mind because it's not delivered in a certain amount of time. Instead, just keep checking on it. The status may be still processing but know for sure that one day it will be delivered.

Remember this:

Job 42:12-13 (KJV) "So the LORD blessed the latter end of Job more than his beginning: for he had fourteen thousand sheep, and six thousand camels, and a thousand yoke of oxen, and a thousand she asses. He had also seven sons and three daughters."

In a Place Called There…

_____
_____
_____
_____
_____
_____
_____
_____
_____
_____

Grow Where God Plants You

    Staying put and growing where God plants you will have favorable results; this will produce stability, focus and accomplishments to be completed. Everyone would like to achieve something in their lives. People who live within their own limitations and parameters may face consequences because of their own ways and choices. When staying in these specific boundaries the decisions that are made typically don't involve surrendering to God's will but according to the natural, how they see things and feel. Moving in this direction can cause confusion, havoc, unorganized and sometimes trouble in our lives. We can't follow to fulfill God's purpose and His will unless we have dealt with ourselves in learning how to surrender.

    Yes, sometimes when you are replanted it can hurt, it's uncomfortable, but it's also humbling. I'm not an expert in gardening but I do have a general idea of how it works. One thing I've observed regarding gardening is that after you purchase the plant it probably would need to be replanted because it has over-grown the capacity space given. For a plan to grow healthy it must have the proper care. Some plants may need sunlight only, while other plants do better in shade only or partial shade. Some plants may need to be watered daily, while other plants will need watering every so often.

    This is exactly how God handles us when we desire to grow and expand in His kingdom. The reasons or purpose God plants an individual is to give the person more space to grow healthy spiritually. When we grow healthy spiritually there is a better understanding of how God operates in our lives on different levels. We learn to completely trust Him, and you can say with confidence that you know He's got it. Where God plants an individual is not necessarily where the person will end up.

Sometimes He places us in areas for preparation to where He is taking us. That preparation may be in a physical, mentally or spiritual sense in order to comply with His will.

~True Story~

During the challenging time of transitioning out of a failed marriage and dealing with the cause and effect of being married to a pastor, when things fell apart there was no place for me to worship. I became acquainted with my church and grew tremendously spiritually and physically adapt ever since I was a young adult. God has done some amazing things during my walk with my church organization, and I gained a new family in the kingdom of God.

My church is an international church, after 28 years of laboring with people, visiting different church locations, gaining strong relationships across the globe, appreciating my church history, loving and embracing it's doctrine, I found myself temporary being planted within another organization. Although this decision was based on the scandal and the position of being a pastor's wife, I really needed to worship somewhere where no one knew anything about me, my situation, my pain, my past and who I might be connected to; they needed to know nothing at all. In the area where I lived was a small town and news traveled fast. So, I needed, as well as desired, a strong, powerful anointed church where I could become part of and connected to. The church did not have to be a perfect place to worship, but it had to be a place that was familiar with spiritual warfare with knowledge and evidence of powerful breakthroughs.

My first decision was to go to a church located in Baltimore, Maryland because my daughter was a student at Morgan State University during that time. The distance was reasonable, from Pennsylvania to Maryland and the church was a good place where no one knew or recognized me. The only issue was that I didn't feel no area for growth.

I began to attend a church in the Philadelphia area named Victory Christian Center under the leadership of Apostle Jimmie A. Ellis, III. During this time, I lived in Mechanicsburg, PA, which was about two hours away from Philadelphia. For approximately two years I traveled every Wednesday evening for bible study and every Sunday morning attending both the 8:00am service and the 11:30am service and any other special service the church would have. Being planted there allowed me to see some things about myself that I was not aware of or realized before. There were personal, intimate, deep things that needed to be corrected so that growth and development could take place. Even though I didn't understand it during that time, the purpose of being replanted was to make me more valuable and for the master's use, even more in the kingdom of God.

~Here's the Thing...~

Each of us has a purpose in which God has for us. No one is destined to stay on the same level, to grow is all within the plan of God. There are many examples of opportunities of grow such as relocating to a different neighborhood or state, changing titles or positions at work, or changing churches worshipping with a different group of believers to name a few. When God is doing the planting, your growth blossoms in such a beauty that can only be noticed everywhere you go.

Remember this:

2 Peter 3:18 (KJV) *"But grow in grace, and in the knowledge of our Lord and Saviour Jesus Christ. To him be glory both now and forever."* Amen'.

In a Place Called There...

Fresh Focus

When there is something fresh it brings a sense of renewal. There is one thing in common that fresh sheets, fresh cut flowers, fresh clothes from the dryer, and fresh cut grass have in common. That is the experience of freshness. When freshness is experienced it will change a negative attitude to a positive attitude. Experiencing freshness can change the course of the day.

One of the most powerful things we can have in life is our experience. We can learn from many things, but there is nothing more valuable than learning from our own experiences. When you have experience in something, you already have a general idea of what to expect. We can ponder the mistakes and have another chance to correct them or expound on the current success and make it greater.

There are times when we can experience favorable results in life but for some reason or another, our mindset does not change, until God changes it. The circumstance hasn't changed. Someone could suffer from an illness, brokenness, still single, widowed or divorced, and bring a new mindset that will give strength to move on, regardless. Once that new way of thinking is changed and embraced, what follows next is the enjoyment of something fresh.

~True Story~

In the beginning of my unplanned transition it was very difficult for me to move forward. When I had no other choice but to relocate, I took everything I could with me. I packed items such as furniture, clothes and pictures that had a sentimental value to me. The problem with keeping these items is that it captivated me in the past. Each item caused me to remember things that I needed to get away from in order to move forward. Once I decided to let go and stop trying to save my marriage, my house, my job and family, things became clear to me that I wasn't living up to my full potential.

Initially, I couldn't see it before or understand it, but now I get it: What was lost in the past cannot be compared to the greater of what will be restored. Glory to God!

In a Place Called There...

_____
_____
_____
_____
_____
_____
_____
_____
_____

Be Still

    We live in a time where trouble is on every hand. It seems the day can't end without dealing with some sort of crisis. Once the crisis introduces itself, some people may go into fear and panic mode, while others may go into resolution mode. In either direction, the-end result is filled with anxiety, worry, frustration and stress.

    I have observed many circumstances whether it was reality or not, that has caused some level of chaos. The response of the incident was often dramatic. In some cases, people may scream or cry, while others' minds are racing, trying to figure out what to do. During these observations it is rare to see calm or stillness from the beginning of a situation.

    What does it mean to *be still*? To remain still, calm, quiet, both physically and mentally. Also, to be still is to snap out of it; stop; or wake up. Sometimes we can react too quickly. After we react shortly thereafter or later, we then realize that things could very well have balanced themselves out if we would have just kept still.

~~True Story~

    I'm the oldest of two sets of twin sisters and a brother. Needless, to say the least, my mother's hands were full. Every day she would start her day at 5:00am and conclude at 8:00pm. Our household was under a strict routine in order to get things accomplished for that day.

I was raised to know how to multi-task and be proactive in order to resolve issues. For many years my approach was to jump in front of the cart (speaking figuratively), so you can imagine that for me, to be still, is a process. With a conscientious effort regarding time, prayer and wisdom, I'm learning to be still because I now understand it can save me from frustration, embarrassment and unnecessary stress.

<u>Remember this</u>:

Psalm 46:10 (KJV) "Be still and know that I am God: I will be exalted among the heathen, I will be exalted in the earth."

In a Place Called There…

_____
_____
_____
_____
_____
_____
_____
_____
_____
_____

Living My Best Life

We will never get too old to do anything great. Many people have tendencies to focus on the number that's concerning their age and not the maturity. When we age, we then mature. Anyone can celebrate a birthday and their age will change but growing in maturity is over a process of time.

The first half of our lives can be considered ~~as~~ a preparation. When we reach a certain age most of our mistakes were made; we gained experience and achieved accomplishments. It's during this season where we have lived and learned. There are some things we may seek God for that He won't answer until we are ready for it. In order to live our best life, we must move forward, pursue opportunities and embrace new experiences. Make it a point to reach new strives every day.

~True Story~

The first half of my life consisted of work and church. There was hardly any time to enjoy anything of leisure. My life was consumed with the demands of church leadership, employment and family. While stuck in this routine, it robbed me of other life experiences. The outcome of this trial has helped me to learn to breathe and live a little.

<u>Remember this</u>:

Haggai 2:9 (KJV) "The glory of this latter house shall be greater than of the former, saith the Lord of hosts: and in this place will I give peace, saith the Lord of hosts."

In a Place Called There...

www.ingramcontent.com/pod-product-compliance
Lightning Source LLC
Chambersburg PA
CBHW070434010526
44118CB00014B/2036